Dangerous Animals

Rebecca Gilpin

Designed by Will Dawes, Katrina Fearn,
Michelle Lawrence and Zoe Waring
Illustrated by Patrizia Donaera

Additional illustrations by Tim Haggerty
Reading consultant: Alison Kelly
Animal consultant: Professor Stuart West, University of Oxford

Contents

3 Watch out...
4 Stay away!
6 Hunting for food
8 Teamwork
10 After dark
12 Hidden dangers
14 Fast and furious
16 Big bruisers
18 Shark attack
20 Scary seas
22 Vicious venom
24 Don't touch!
26 Deadly diseases
28 Animals in danger
30 Glossary
31 Usborne Quicklinks
32 Index

Watch out...

Animals can be dangerous for lots of different reasons. They may be scared, hungry or even protecting their family.

This rattlesnake is rattling its scaly tail. It is a warning that it may attack.

Stay away!

Animals can be dangerous when they are protecting their babies or the place where they live.

A mother polar bear looks after her cubs until they can look after themselves.

A male bear tries to attack the cubs. The mother protects them.

She scares the bear away and her cubs are safe for the moment.

Some animals defend the area where they live and hunt. This area is called their territory.

Tigers fight other tigers that come into their territory. Sometimes they fight until one of them dies.

Hunting for food

Animals that eat meat kill other animals. Some use special skills to catch their prey.

Cheetahs sprint after prey such as antelopes and then pull them to the ground.

Brown bears wait in streams to catch leaping salmon.

A boa constrictor coils around its prey and squeezes it to death.

A tiger's stripes are like camouflage – it can sneak up on its prey without being seen.

An eagle swoops and snatches a fish in its sharp claws.

Scorpions sting and stun prey with poison in their tails.

Teamwork

Some animals live in groups and hunt as a team, so that they can kill bigger animals.

Wolves live and hunt in family groups called packs. They kill animals such as deer and moose.

Wolves can follow the smell of their prey through the snow.

Female lions hunt together. They chase a zebra away from its herd and drag it to the ground.

One lion bites the zebra's throat and holds on until it stops breathing.

The lions all feed on the dead zebra.

After dark

When night falls, some animals have special ways of finding prey in the dark.

A pit viper has two deep holes in its face that feel heat given off by other animals.

This means that small animals can't even hide from the viper in the dark.

An owl's large eyes let it see really well, even when there is almost no light.

It flies quietly, then swoops and grabs small animals in its sharp claws.

Hidden dangers

Some animals hide and wait for prey, instead of chasing it.

Leopards climb trees, then leap down onto animals that pass by.

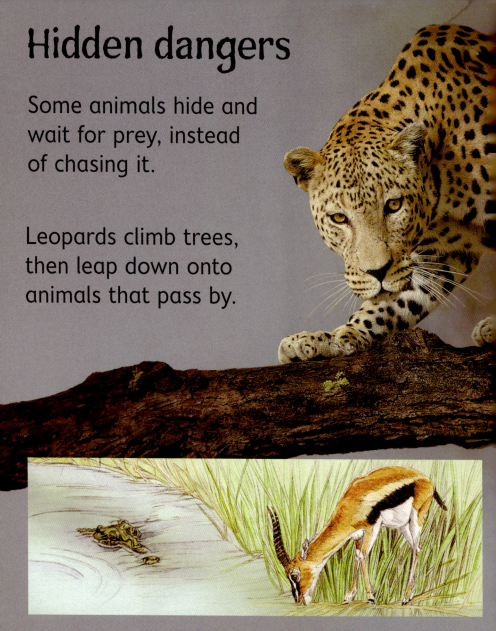

A crocodile swims in a river, with only part of its head showing.

A gazelle drinks from the river but doesn't see the crocodile.

The crocodile lunges up and grabs the gazelle in its jaws.

It rolls over and pulls the gazelle under the water to drown it.

Fast and furious

Some animals move very fast when they are hunting or if something surprises them.

A peregrine falcon spots a pigeon and dives down to attack it.

It crashes into the pigeon at an amazing speed and kills it.

The falcon eats the dead pigeon on the ground.

A hunting cheetah can run three times faster than the fastest person.

Bears can run very fast. They sometimes chase people who catch them by surprise.

Big bruisers

Big animals can be dangerous because of their size and strength.

Hippos are huge. They sometimes kill people who come too close.

Hippos lie in rivers to keep cool.

Male hippos often fight over territory. They attack with their huge teeth.

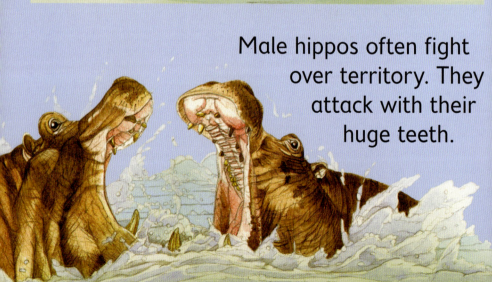

African elephants are the biggest animals that live on land. They often charge at other animals to scare them away.

Shark attack

Sharks are the fiercest hunters in the sea. They can hear and smell prey from a long way away.

Great white sharks hunt big fish, seals and dolphins. Sometimes they attack people too, but this is rare.

This great white shark is breaking through the surface of the sea to attack a seal.

Tiger sharks have a very good sense of smell.

A tiger shark smells blood coming from an injured turtle.

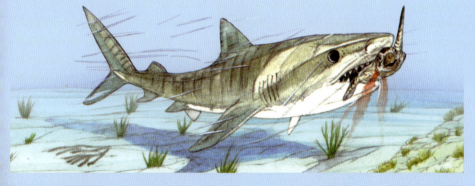

The shark attacks. It crunches the turtle with its strong jaws and sharp teeth.

Scary seas

Sharks aren't the only killers in the sea. Lots of other dangerous creatures live there too.

A blue-ringed octopus is only as big as a golf ball, but its poison can kill a person in minutes.

It turns bright yellow with blue markings when it is about to attack.

Box jellyfish sting small fish to death with their tentacles. Their sting can also kill people.

A stonefish has poisonous spines along its back. It can kill people who step on it by accident.

Electric rays hide in the sand and give an electric shock if they are touched.

Cone snails inject fish with deadly poison, then swallow them whole.

Vicious venom

Some snakes and spiders have sharp fangs filled with poisonous venom. Their venom can be very dangerous to people.

Spitting cobras shoot venom at an attacker's eyes to blind it...

...then they strike with their fangs and inject more deadly venom.

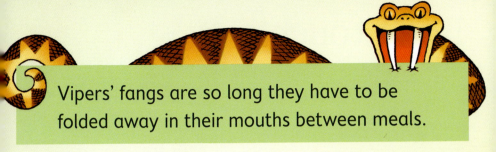

Vipers' fangs are so long they have to be folded away in their mouths between meals.

A Sydney funnel-web spider sits inside its web and waits for prey to pass by.

A beetle steps on a thread linked to the web, and the spider feels the web move.

The spider scuttles out. It sinks its fangs into the beetle and injects venom into it.

Don't touch!

Some animals have bright markings or sharp spines that tell other animals to stay away.

The bright skin of a poison arrow frog warns attackers that it is deadly poisonous.

Some people in South America use poison from frogs on their arrows when they go hunting.

Lionfish
have spines
with poison
on the ends.

They swim in the sea around coral reefs looking for small fish to eat.

Sometimes a diver touches a lionfish by accident and gets stung by its spines.

Deadly diseases

Some animals are dangerous because they spread diseases.

A few female mosquitoes can spread a deadly disease called malaria when they bite people.

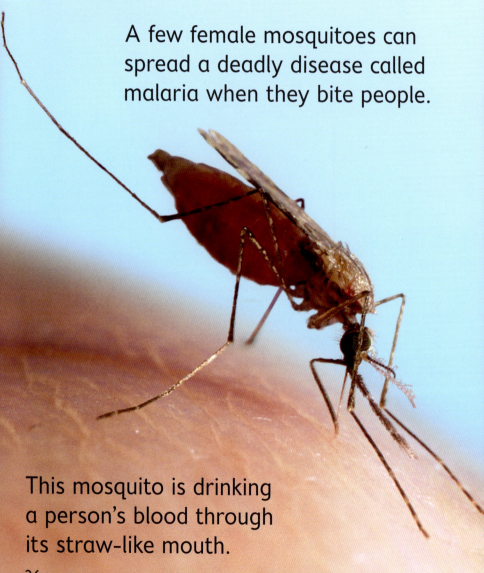

This mosquito is drinking a person's blood through its straw-like mouth.

Rats live in most places where people live. They carry diseases that can make people very ill.

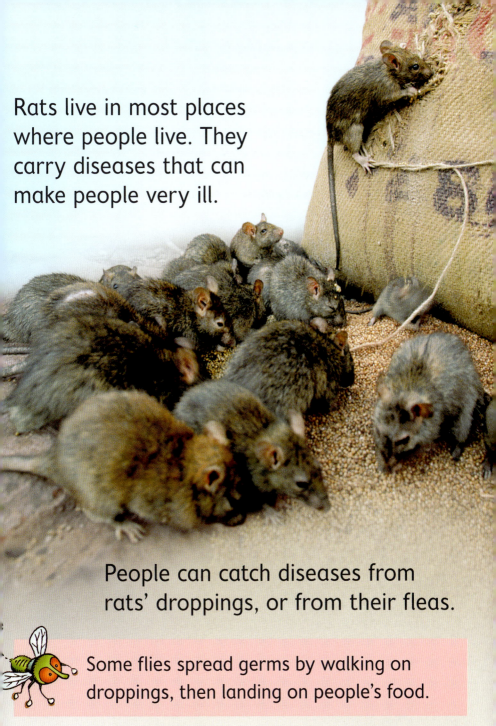

People can catch diseases from rats' droppings, or from their fleas.

Some flies spread germs by walking on droppings, then landing on people's food.

Animals in danger

People can be even more dangerous to animals than animals are to people.

Hunters shoot and kill wild animals for their fur, skins and horns.

People cut down trees in the places where animals live, and use the land for houses and farming.

Sharks, fish and seabirds are killed by oil leaking from damaged ships.

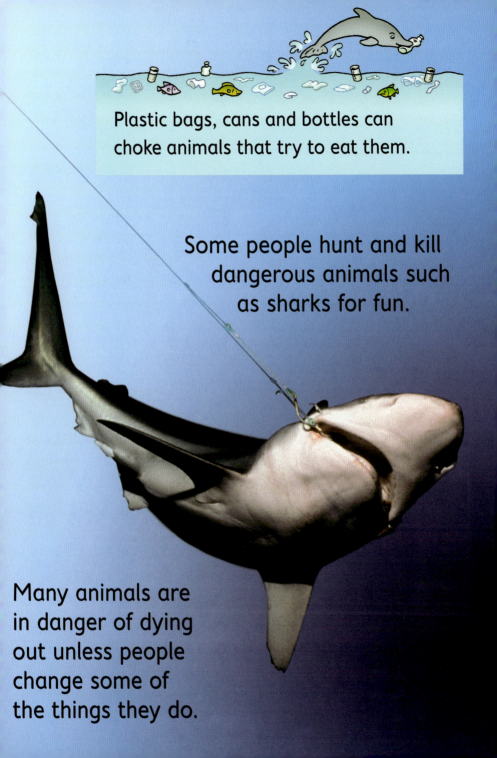

Plastic bags, cans and bottles can choke animals that try to eat them.

Some people hunt and kill dangerous animals such as sharks for fun.

Many animals are in danger of dying out unless people change some of the things they do.

Glossary

Here are some of the words in this book you might not know. This page tells you what they mean.

 hunt - to look for, catch and kill animals, usually to eat.

 territory - an area where an animal lives and hunts.

 prey - animals that are hunted and eaten by other animals.

 poisonous - something poisonous can make you ill or kill you.

 venom - a poisonous liquid that some animals use to stun and kill.

 fangs - sharp pointed teeth. Some animals' fangs are filled with venom.

 tentacles - long parts of a jellyfish that can sting and even kill.

Usborne Quicklinks

Would you like to find out more about dangerous animals? Visit Usborne Quicklinks for links to websites with videos, facts and activities about snakes, sharks and other amazing creatures.

Go to **usborne.com/Quicklinks** and type in the keywords "**beginners dangerous animals**". Make sure you ask a grown-up before going online.

Notes for grown-ups

Please read the internet safety guidelines at Usborne Quicklinks with your child. Children should be supervised online. The websites are regularly reviewed and the links at Usborne Quicklinks are updated. However, Usborne Publishing is not responsible and does not accept liability for the content or availability of any website other than its own.

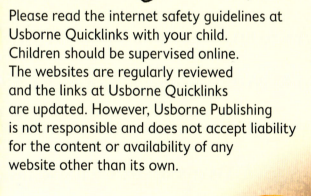

Scorpions come out at night and hunt for bugs.

Index

bears, 4, 6, 15
beetles, 23
birds, 7, 11, 14, 28
cheetahs, 6-7, 15
crocodiles, 12-13
elephants, 17
fangs, 22, 23, 30
fish, 6, 7, 18, 21, 25, 28
fleas, 27
flies, 27
hippos, 16
hunting, 5, 6-13, 14, 15, 18, 19, 24, 28, 30
leopards, 12-13
lions, 9
mosquitoes, 26
poison, 7, 20, 21, 22, 23, 24, 25, 30
prey, 6, 7, 8, 10, 11, 12-13, 14, 18, 19, 21, 23, 30
rats, 27
scorpions, 7, 31
sharks, 18-19, 20, 28, 29, 31
snakes, 3, 6, 10, 22, 23, 31
spiders, 22, 23
tentacles, 21, 30
territory, 5, 16, 30
tigers, 5, 7
venom, 22-23, 30
wolves, 8

Acknowledgements

Photographic manipulation by John Russell

Photo credits

The publishers are grateful to the following for permission to reproduce material:
cover © Digital Vision; **p.1** © Steve Bloom Images/Alamy Stock Photo; **p.2-3** © franzfoto.com/Alamy Stock Photo; **p.5** © John Conrad/Corbis Documentary/Getty Images; **p.6-7** © Steve Bloom Images/Alamy Stock Photo; **p.8** © Jeff Vanuga; **p.11** © Eureka/Alamy Stock Photo; **p.12-13** © M. Watson/Ardea; **p.15** © Johnny Johnson/The Image Bank/Getty Images; **p.17** © Steve Bloom Images/Alamy Stock Photo; **p.18** © Fabrice Bettex/Alamy Stock Photo; **p.19** © Michael Pitts/naturepl; **p.20** © John Lewis/Natural Visions; **p.22** © Digital Vision; **p.24** © Buddy Mayes/Alamy Stock Photo; **p.25** © Ron Steiner/Alamy; **p.26** © Sinclair Stammer/SPL; **p.27** © John Downer/Stone/Getty Images; **p.29** © Jeff Rotman/naturepl; **p.31** © Digital Vision.

Every effort has been made to trace and acknowledge ownership of copyright. If any rights have been omitted, the publishers offer to rectify this in any subsequent editions following notification.

This edition first published in 2021 by Usborne Publishing Limited, 83-85 Saffron Hill, London EC1N 8RT, United Kingdom. usborne.com Copyright © 2021, 2008 Usborne Publishing Limited. The name Usborne and the Balloon logo are registered trade marks of Usborne Publishing Limited. All rights reserved. No part of this publication may be reproduced, stored in a retrieval system, or transmitted in any form or by any means without the prior permission of the publisher.
First published in America 2021. This edition published 2024. UE.